the world of Native
AMERICANS

First published in Great Britain in 1997
by Macdonald Young Books
an imprint of Wayland Publishers Limited

Macdonald Young Books
61 Western Road
Hove
East Sussex BN3 1JD

Art Direction and Design
McRae Books Ltd,
Florence, Italy

You can find Macdonald Young Books
on the internet at:
http://www.wayland.co.uk

A CIP catalogue record for this book
is available from the British Library

ISBN 0 7500 2276 0

Printed and bound in Portugal
by Edições ASA

Marion Wood

Marion Wood was educated at the Universities of St Andrews and Leicester. She has held the position of Assistant Keeper of Ethnography at Leeds City Museum and at the Horniman Museum, London. She is currently Assistant Curator of East Fife Museum Service in Scotland. She has a long-standing interest in the material culture of the Native Americans and has written and lectured widely on the subject.

Colin Taylor

Colin Taylor obtained his Ph.D from the University of Essex. He has studied the culture of the North American Indian for almost forty years and has written extensively on the subject. Dr Taylor lectures regularly, both in the United Kingdom and in North America.

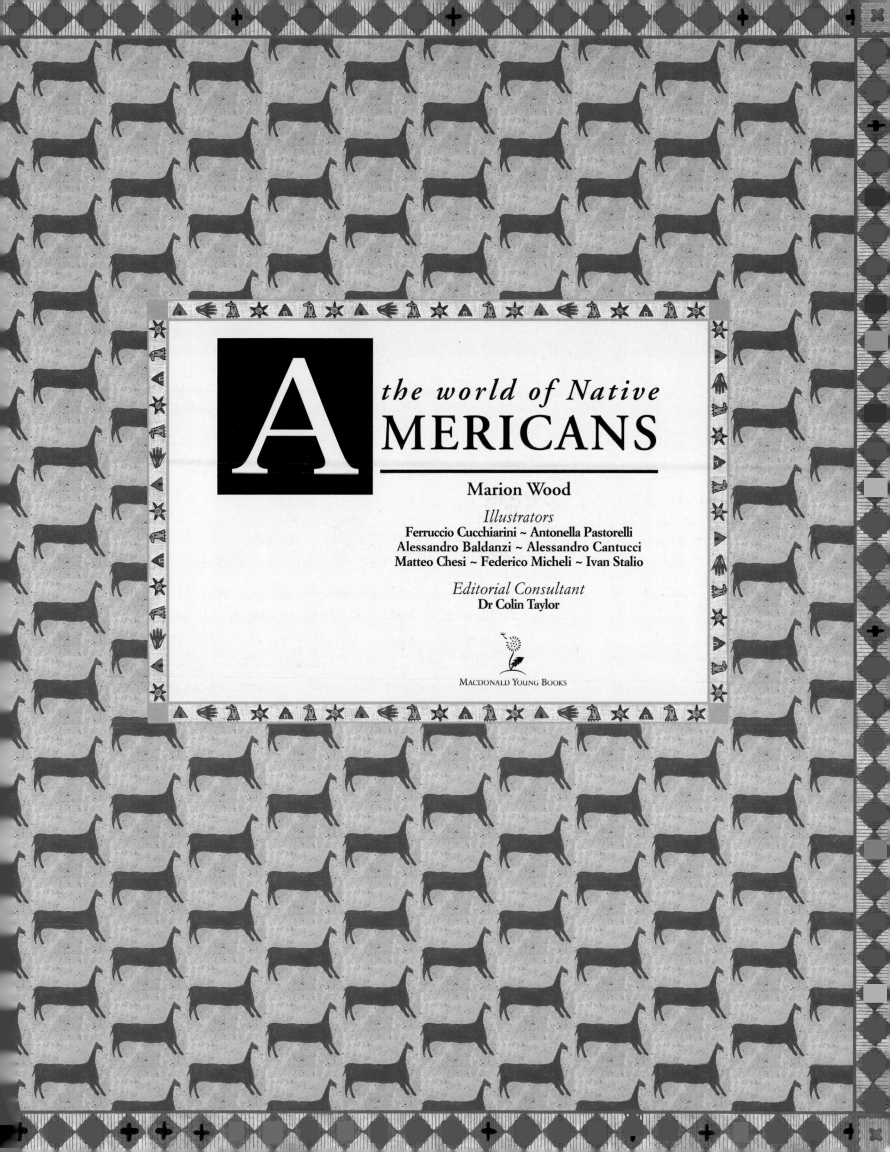

A the world of Native MERICANS

Marion Wood

Illustrators
Ferruccio Cucchiarini ~ Antonella Pastorelli
Alessandro Baldanzi ~ Alessandro Cantucci
Matteo Chesi ~ Federico Micheli ~ Ivan Stalio

Editorial Consultant
Dr Colin Taylor

MACDONALD YOUNG BOOKS

CONTENTS

INTRODUCTION

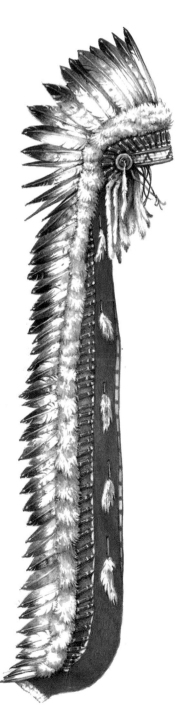

The popular image of Native Americans is of painted warriors in feathers and buckskin, hunting buffalo on horseback. But this picture does not fit all Native Americans. In fact, it only fits one group of Plains Indians at a late point in their history, when white people had already arrived to alter their lives in many ways – by bringing in horses, for instance.

Viking sagas reveal that Columbus's voyages to the Americas were not the first made by Europeans. Around AD 1000, Leif Eriksson and his fellow Norsemen had explored the coasts of Nova Scotia and Newfoundland. They even settled there briefly, though they left little trace of their visit.

Columbus arrived in America by mistake. He had intended to find a new route to India, and when he reached the Bahamas in 1492, he thought that he had. That is why we call the islands where he landed the West Indies and why Native Americans are still known as Indians. But the voyages of Columbus were different from those of the Norsemen, for they opened the way to the exploitation of the whole continent. Columbus himself had clear views on how the Native Americans ought to be treated. Reporting back to his master, the King of Spain, he wrote, 'They became marvellously friendly to us… They should make good servants.'

Neither the Norsemen nor Columbus actually 'discovered' America. By the time Columbus arrived, there were millions of people already living there. It was their ancestors who had really discovered America thousands of years earlier. Unfortunately, we still know very little about these early people – not even their real names. The Hopewell people, for example, are named after the farmer on whose land their burial mounds were found.

Since Native Americans did not have a written language, they could not leave behind an account of their own stories. Much of our information about them comes from the writing of white people, many of whom, sadly, could not appreciate people whose way of life was different from their own. To many European settlers, Native Americans were 'savages', occupying valuable land which they did not use properly.

Native Americans were not one people with an unchanging lifestyle. There were hundreds of different tribes, whose way of life changed over the centuries. The coming of the Europeans in the fifteenth century, with their technology and diseases, brought about the most devastating changes of all.

THE MAMMOTH HUNTERS

The ancestors of the first Americans emigrated from North-Eastern Asia during the last Ice Age, possibly around 25,000 years ago. At that time, large areas of the earth's surface were covered with huge sheets of ice up to three metres thick. So much water was frozen into the ice that all over the world the level of the sea dropped. In some areas, this resulted in the sea-bed becoming exposed as dry land. One such area was the Bering Strait. The early settlers were not very numerous. This was no rampaging horde sweeping across the country. Unlike those who came from Europe many centuries later, these first Americans were motivated by their need for survival, not by any thoughts of conquest. As they moved slowly out of Asia towards the still unpopulated American continent, the same conditions prevailed on both sides of the land bridge and there were no barriers or frontiers for them to cross.

CROSSING THE BERING STRAIT

Palaeo-Indian hunter

ASIA

BERING STRAIT

NORTH AMERICA

Prehistoric bison

For much of the Ice Age, the Bering Strait, the stretch of water that today separates America from Asia was a grassy plain, up to a thousand kilometres wide, joining the two continents together. This vast bridge of land, which historians have called Beringia, was a cold and windswept place, but it was free from ice and there was enough vegetation to provide grazing for the herds of large Ice Age mammals that roamed over it. In their wake came nomadic hunters who depended on these great animals for food.

Spear with chipped stone blade mounted on a wooden shaft.

Ice Age Mammals
These included mammoths, mastodons, woolly rhinoceros, bison, camels and horses – all much larger than their present-day counterparts.

Over thousands of years, the hunters drifted across the Bering Strait and into what is now Alaska. They travelled on foot in small family groups – people of all ages from elderly grandparents to tiny babies – constantly following the game herds. The hunters also gathered edible plants and berries to eat, but they did not plant any crops.

As the Ice Age came to an end, the glaciers melted and the hunters were able to move slowly down into the heart of the continent and beyond. Behind them, the sea rose to its present level, covering the land bridge and separating America from Asia for ever.

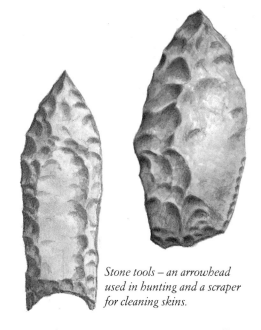

Stone tools – an arrowhead used in hunting and a scraper for cleaning skins.

Dogs

The first Americans had no domestic animals except for their dogs. These were large wolf-like creatures which they kept for hunting and protection and to help them carry their belongings.

An Early Native American Hunting Village

We can only guess at how the first Americans lived, since they have left little evidence behind. They would have worn warm clothing made from the skins of the animals they hunted. They must have been able to build shelters and make the tools and weapons that they needed to stay alive.

THE SETTLING OF NORTH AMERICA

With the ending of the Ice Age, the climate of North America became warmer and plant and animal life changed. In some areas, deserts appeared. In others, grasslands gave way to thick forests. The large game herds dwindled and some animals, like the mammoth, became extinct. In order to survive, the hunters had to adapt to the changing environment. Some developed weapons and traps for hunting smaller animals or for catching birds or fish. Others turned to eating more plant food and, in time, learned to cultivate and irrigate the soil and became farmers. They learned to make the best use of the materials that their environment offered, and so learned to work with stone, wood, bone, antler and skins, and to make pottery and weave cloth.

Some of the hunters remained nomadic, others settled down and built villages and towns. By the time Europeans arrived, the Native Americans had spread all over the continent. In North America alone, they were divided into hundreds of tribes, living in many different ways and speaking more languages than were spoken in the whole of Europe. Historians and anthropologists often classify Indian ways of life according to environment and have divided North America into what are known as culture areas. There can be much diversity within a culture area, but, in general, the tribes living in a similar environment did tend to have a great many things in common.

The North-West Coast
Rocky coastal strip with many islands and inlets. Forested mountains behind. Mild climate with high rainfall.

The South-West
Mountains and forests to the north, flat grassland and semi-desert to the south. Low rainfall.

NORTH-AMERICAN CULTURAL AREAS
1 The South-Eastern Woodlands
2 The North-Eastern Woodlands
3 The Northern Forests
4 The Great Plains
5 The North-West Coast
6 The Plateau and Basin
7 California
8 The South-West

California
Fertile coastal area with grasslands, wooded hills and river valleys.

5

6

7

8

The Northern Forests
Thick forests and treeless tundra, with mountains to the west. Harsh climate, very cold in winter.

The North-Eastern Woodlands
Low, rolling countryside with woods, lakes and rivers. High rainfall.

The Great Plains
Flat, treeless prairies and grasslands. Low rainfall.

The Plateau and Basin
Forested mountains, deep river valleys, windswept plains and semi-desert to the south.

The South-Eastern Woodlands
A fairly flat landscape, with thick forests. Semi-tropical and swampy to the south. High rainfall.

3

4

2

1

THE MOUND BUILDERS

When white settlers first pushed into the Midwestern states at the end of the eighteenth century, they found thousands of mysterious mounds of earth. In the Ohio Valley alone, there were 10,000 of these mounds, all apparently man-made. Some were only a few metres high, while others were huge and loomed over the countryside. Some of the dome-shaped mounds contained burials, and farmers who ploughed into them found fragments of bone, pottery, shell and metalwork scattered across their fields. Other ridge-shaped mounds seemed to form enclosures. Strangest of all were those shaped like human figures, gigantic birds or writhing serpents. Who had built these strange earthworks, now abandoned and overgrown? The Indians who lived in the area, such as the Cherokee, knew little about them except that they had been there for as long as anyone could remember. Some had ancient trees growing on them, showing that what lay underneath had not been disturbed for hundreds of years.

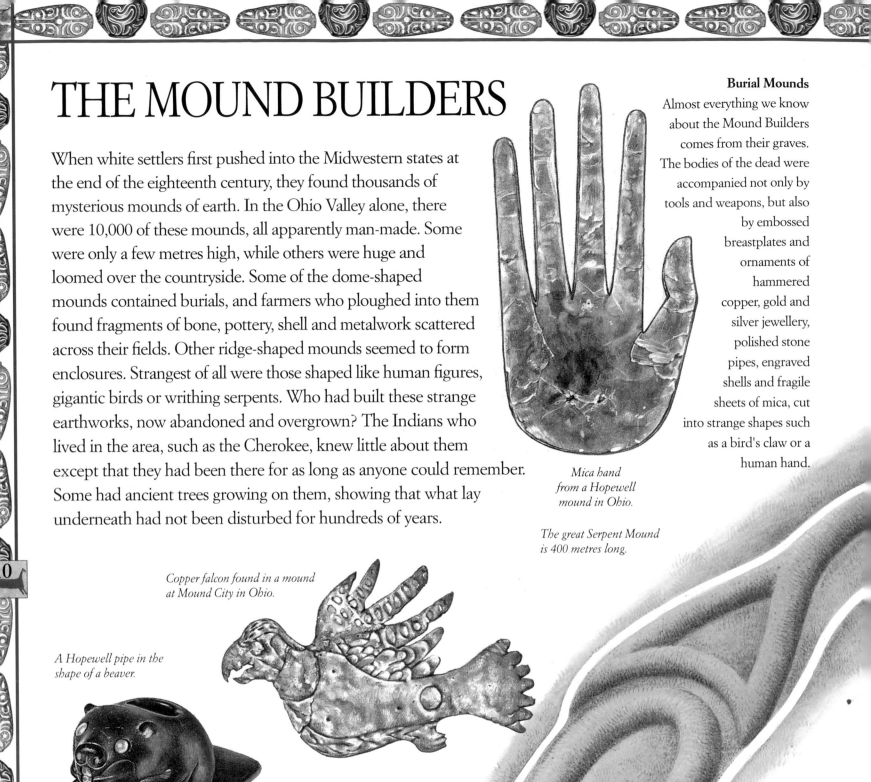

Mica hand from a Hopewell mound in Ohio.

The great Serpent Mound is 400 metres long.

Burial Mounds

Almost everything we know about the Mound Builders comes from their graves. The bodies of the dead were accompanied not only by tools and weapons, but also by embossed breastplates and ornaments of hammered copper, gold and silver jewellery, polished stone pipes, engraved shells and fragile sheets of mica, cut into strange shapes such as a bird's claw or a human hand.

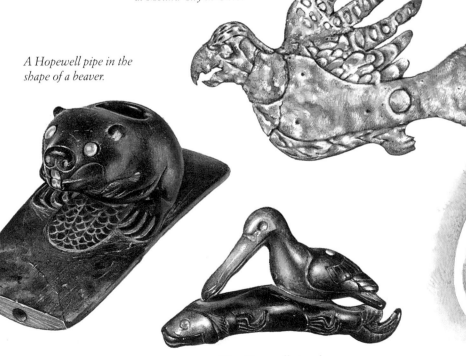

Copper falcon found in a mound at Mound City in Ohio.

A Hopewell pipe in the shape of a beaver.

Tiny Hopewell pipe shows a spoonbill sitting on a fish.

A copper fish from a Hopewell tomb in Ohio.

The Great Serpent Mound

Since the eighteenth century, many hundreds of mounds have been ploughed flat or built on by modern cities, but some have survived. The great Serpent Mound continues to wind its 400-metre length along an Ohio hilltop, still mysterious, its purpose unknown.

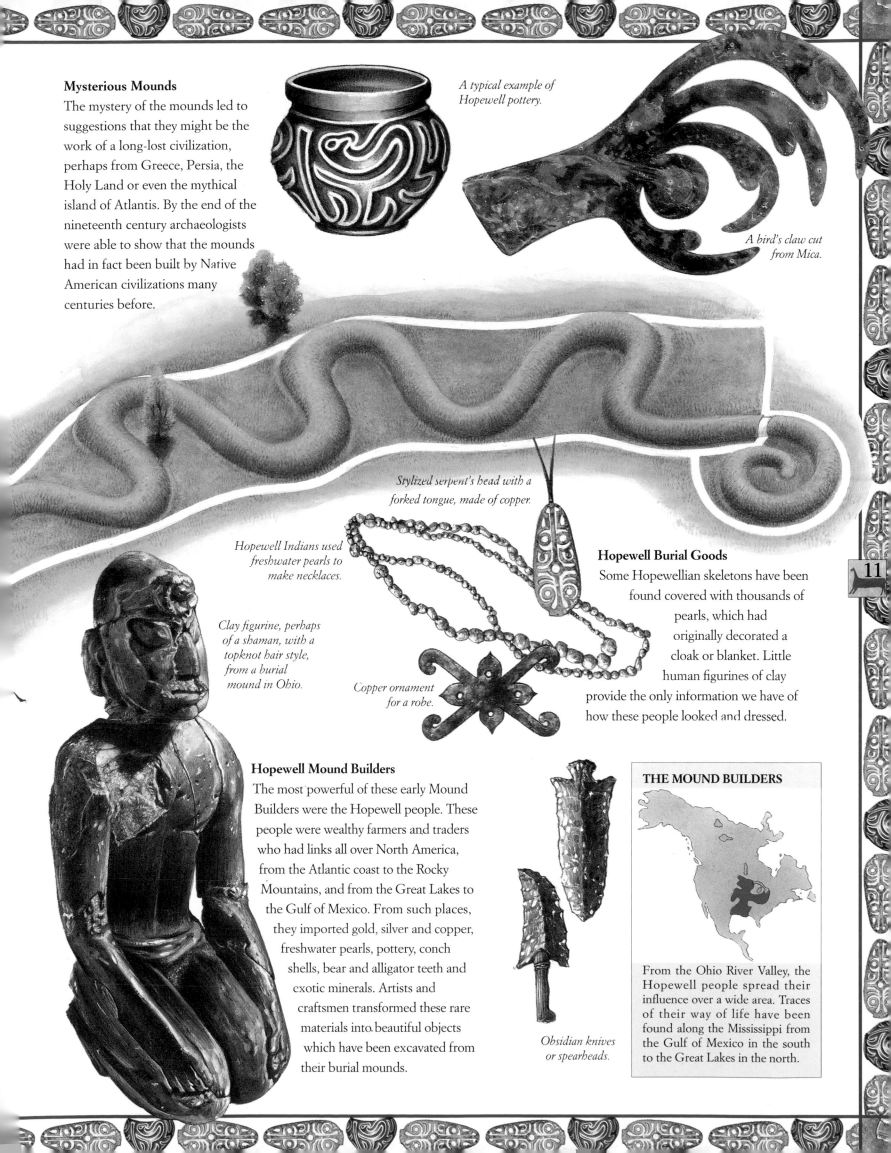

Mysterious Mounds

The mystery of the mounds led to suggestions that they might be the work of a long-lost civilization, perhaps from Greece, Persia, the Holy Land or even the mythical island of Atlantis. By the end of the nineteenth century archaeologists were able to show that the mounds had in fact been built by Native American civilizations many centuries before.

A typical example of Hopewell pottery.

A bird's claw cut from Mica.

Stylized serpent's head with a forked tongue, made of copper.

Hopewell Indians used freshwater pearls to make necklaces.

Clay figurine, perhaps of a shaman, with a topknot hair style, from a burial mound in Ohio.

Copper ornament for a robe.

Hopewell Burial Goods

Some Hopewellian skeletons have been found covered with thousands of pearls, which had originally decorated a cloak or blanket. Little human figurines of clay provide the only information we have of how these people looked and dressed.

Hopewell Mound Builders

The most powerful of these early Mound Builders were the Hopewell people. These people were wealthy farmers and traders who had links all over North America, from the Atlantic coast to the Rocky Mountains, and from the Great Lakes to the Gulf of Mexico. From such places, they imported gold, silver and copper, freshwater pearls, pottery, conch shells, bear and alligator teeth and exotic minerals. Artists and craftsmen transformed these rare materials into beautiful objects which have been excavated from their burial mounds.

Obsidian knives or spearheads.

THE MOUND BUILDERS

From the Ohio River Valley, the Hopewell people spread their influence over a wide area. Traces of their way of life have been found along the Mississippi from the Gulf of Mexico in the south to the Great Lakes in the north.

THE FIRST TOWNS

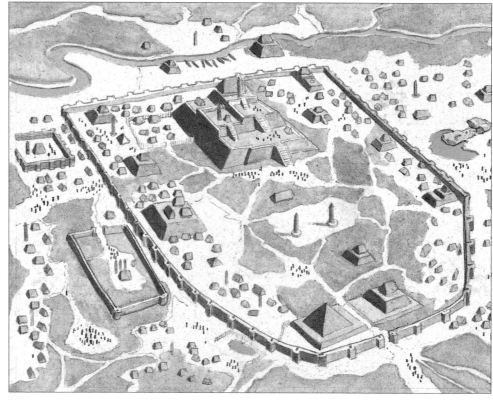

The first towns in North America appeared over a thousand years ago. Cahokia, which stood near the modern city of St Louis, was the greatest of those built in the Mississippi River valley and flourished for nearly seven hundred years.

The most striking feature of this great palisaded city was its many mounds. Some of the smaller ones held storehouses for corn and other crops while larger mounds served as platforms for the houses of the city's more important citizens. Dwarfing them all was the great flat-topped pyramid, known today as Monk's Mound, that was Cahokia's religious and political centre. It covered an area greater than that of any of the Egyptian pyramids and rose in four broad terraces to a height of 30 metres above the city.

A circle of wooden posts near Cahokia is thought to have been an observatory for calculating the best times for planting crops.

Cahokia

In its heyday, around AD 1100, Cahokia covered an area of 13 square kilometres. With over ten thousand people living there, and thousands more living in outlying villages spread along the river valley, it was the largest American city north of Mexico. Indeed, it was not until the nineteenth century that the city of Philadelphia surpassed it in size of population.

Pottery bottle from Cahokia showing a mother nursing her child.

Perhaps the most incredible aspect of Monk's Mound is that it is entirely man-made. The people of Cahokia had neither pack animals nor wheeled vehicles. Every grain of earth must have been carried by the basketful on the backs of the labourers who constructed it.

The building on its topmost level was probably the palace of the Monk's Mound city's ruler, with the homes of important officials on the lower levels. By the time the first European explorers found it, Cahokia's greatness had vanished and it was a ghost city of overgrown mounds.

Pueblo Bonito

Pueblo Bonito was, in effect, a town contained within a single multi-storey building. Five storeys high in all, it rose above its central square like a great D-shaped amphitheatre. Over a thousand people were housed in its eight hundred rooms.

In the South-West, the Anasazi people built a series of large planned towns in New Mexico's Chaco Canyon. The most impressive of these is Pueblo Bonito – 'beautiful town', as Spanish explorers named it. Outside the walls lay large irrigated fields and gardens where the town's inhabitants grew their food crops.

13

Large pottery jar used for transporting and storing water.

Tall cup or pitcher typical of the pottery found at Pueblo Bonito, Chaco Canyon, New Mexico.

Basketry

Baskets are less common than pots on Anasazi sites, but those that are found are often highly decorated and may have had some ceremonial use. At Pueblo Bonito, for example, baskets have been found in graves.

Pottery

Anasazi potters built up their pots by coiling rolls of clay in a spiral fashion, smoothing and shaping as they went along. The finished pots were left to dry before being decorated with bold geometric patterns.

Mesa Verde style mug found at Chaco Canyon.

Pueblo Bonito was not just a farming community. It was a busy commercial centre linked to other towns in the canyon and beyond by a network of roads. Within Pueblo Bonito there were many skilful crafts workers – potters, weavers, makers of basketry and featherwork, workers in turquoise, shell and jet. Merchants from as far away as southern Mexico and the Pacific coast, were drawn to its market-place, bringing with them exotic goods and materials.

The town was also an administrative and religious centre. It had more than thirty kivas – circular underground rooms, accessible only by ladders – where meetings and ceremonies were held.

Elsewhere in the South-West, other Anasazi towns were built into natural recesses high up in the walls of steep-sided canyons. One of the largest, Cliff Palace at Mesa Verde in Colorado, contains over four hundred interconnected rooms on four storeys and must have housed several hundred people.

Anasazi cliff dwellings must rank as some of the most inaccessible homes ever built. At Cliff Palace the canyon floor lies over 200 metres below the houses. Above, there rises 30 metres of sheer cliff. Yet, in order to reach their fields on top of the mesa, the residents of Cliff Palace must have climbed up and down the cliff-face several times a day, laden with tools, baskets and small children. It is still possible to see the finger- and toe-holds which they hacked out of the rock.

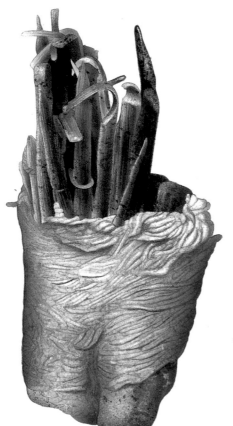

Anasazi basket with carved wooden prayer sticks.

Religion

Without written documents, it is difficult to be sure about Anasazi religious ideas. Archaeological evidence suggests that they may have practised the same sort of rituals as their modern Pueblo descendants.

During the twelfth century, the South-West of North America was devastated by a terrible series of droughts which lasted over fifty years. Unable to carry on farming, the Anasazi began to desert their towns and villages. By the beginning of the fourteenth century, the cliff dwellings, and even the great Pueblo Bonito itself, had been abandoned.

Kivas
The circular openings in front of the houses are the entrances to underground kivas, accessible only by ladder. Kivas are still an important feature of present-day Pueblo villages.

Shell necklace.

Cliff Palace
Nestling under an overhanging rock, Cliff Palace at Mesa Verde, Colorado, is now a ruin, but it once housed hundreds of people. Rising in a series of terraces, the houses were built of sandstone blocks cemented together with mud.

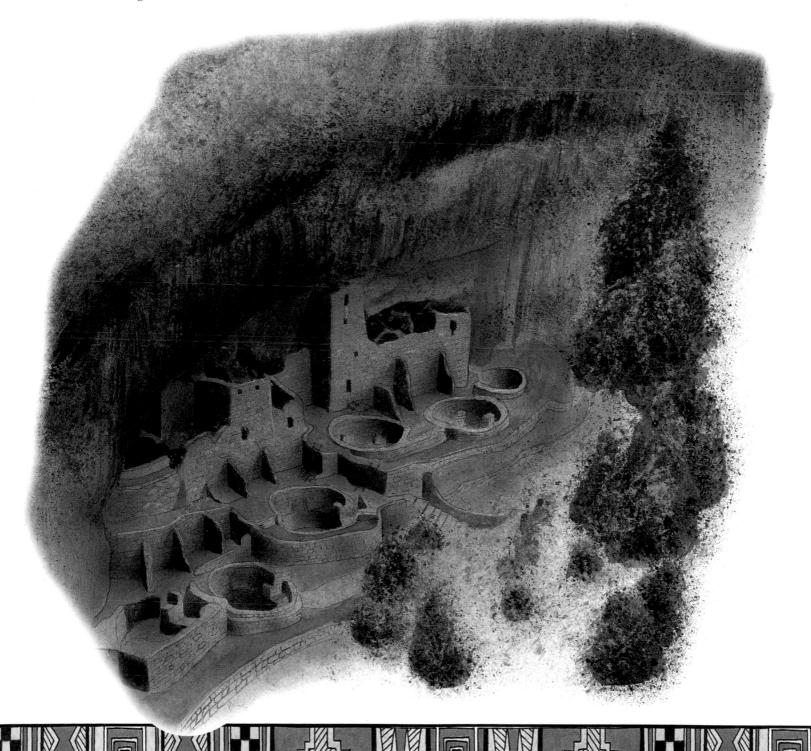

THE SOUTH-EASTERN WOODLANDS

The Mound Builder tradition was still alive in the South-East when Spanish conquistadors first explored the region in the early seventeenth century. Their records describe many well-built towns and villages lining the river valleys. Within each town, great earthen mounds topped with important buildings were grouped around central squares, while beyond lay carefully tended fields of corn, beans and squash. Another important feature of South-Eastern towns were the playing fields for games. All the woodland tribes enjoyed a wide variety of games based on skill or chance – shooting arrows, tossing lances at a rolling stone disk or gambling on which moccasin held a stone or marker. Perhaps the wildest game of all was stickball, the forerunner of lacrosse.

Of all the tribes on the Mississippi River, the Natchez were described as the largest, strongest and proudest. Their palisaded towns were clustered not far from where the present-day city of Natchez now stands. The ruler of the Natchez was a powerful chief known as the Great Sun, who traced his descent from the sun itself. He was revered by his subjects like a god, and lived in isolated splendour.

Feathered staff carried in ceremonial dances.

Games

Southern tribes played lacrosse with two wooden sticks, unlike the modern game which is played with one. The ball was made of deer hair, wrapped with deer hide thongs. The object of the game was to pass or carry a ball to a goal – a single post, or two set at varying distances apart. The game was often very violent, and bloodshed and broken bones were not uncommon. But this ball game was so popular that teams might play for six or eight hours without a break.

Cherokee drum used during dancing ceremonies. The base is made of wood with animal skin stretched over the top.

Flute made of cedar wood.

Chunkey was another popular sport. A player rolled a smooth stone with a hole in the middle along the ground. At the same time, he and the other players threw wooden spears to the point where they thought the stone would stop.

Cherokee dance rattle made from the hollowed-out shell of a pumpkin.

But, like many of the eastern tribes, even the powerful Natchez were not able to withstand the aggressive military force of the European invaders, nor the diseases that they brought with them. By the eighteenth century, their civilization had been wiped out and their towns destroyed.

The remaining tribes – the Choctaw, Cherokee, Chickasaw, Creek and Seminole – survived by adopting European ways and they became known as the 'Five Civilized Tribes'. Yet even this was not enough to save their homelands. In the 1830s, a gold rush, together with the white settlers' greed for land, led to their enforced removal to territory in Oklahoma. The Cherokee refer to this tragic event in their history as the 'Trail of Tears'. Many Seminole resisted the attempts to remove them and scattered groups, too weak to pose a threat, held out in the swamps of the Everglades. Many Seminole still live in Florida today.

The South-Eastern Woodlands was bounded in the east by the Atlantic Ocean and to the south by the Gulf of Mexico. To the west it merged with the Great Plains and to the north with the North-Eastern Woodlands.

Wooden spoons for stirring porridge, and a woven basketry plate.

17

Clothing

This mid-19th century costume shows a mixture of Indian and European materials and styles. Although men still preferred breech-cloth and leggings to trousers, these were now made of European cloth instead of buckskin. The feathered turban is traditional, but the silver band is a European addition.

Food

Corn provided the basis for most meals. The kernels were pounded in a wooden mortar made from a log hollowed out by charring and scraping. Coarse corn meal was boiled into a porridge. More finely ground flour was made into bread, boiled in cornhusk wrappers or baked on hot stones.

Pestle used for grinding corn in a mortar made from a hollowed-out tree trunk.

Baskets and bowls used for preparing and eating food. The ladle is made from the dried skin of a gourd.

THE NORTH-EASTERN WOODLANDS

The Indians who lived in the North-Eastern Woodlands and around the Great Lakes hunted and fished, but the main occupation was farming. The Iroquois in particular were farmers on a grand scale, growing fifteen types of corn, eight types of squash and over sixty types of beans – the plants they called the 'Three Sisters'. As well as farming, people were able to gather a plentiful supply of wild plants, fruit and nuts. The sap of the maple tree was collected in the spring and boiled up to make syrup and sugar. In some areas, wild rice was harvested from shallow lakes and streams.

The Indians of the North-Eastern Woodlands lived along the rivers, lakes and seashore in the woodland areas stretching from Lake Superior in the north-west to the Atlantic coast in the east. They merged with the peoples of the South-Eastern woodlands along the Mississippi River in the south.

The 'Three Sisters' – corn, beans and squash.

18

Husk Face Society mask.

Masks

Sometimes the festivals were combined with ceremonies to cure illness and disease. These were carried out by various secret societies, such as the False Face Society, whose members wore grotesque wooden masks traditionally carved from living trees. The False Faces represented strange beings glimpsed in the forest or in dreams. The society is still a popular one and has many members today. Once or twice a year, they visit all the houses in the area and perform ceremonies to clear disease.

Festivals

There were a number of agricultural festivals throughout the year. There was the Maple Festival, held in spring to celebrate the rising of the maple sap, the Seed Planting Festival, the Wild Strawberry Festival to mark the ripening of the first fruit, the Green Corn Festival to celebrate the ripening of the corn, beans and squash, and the Harvest Festival. The longest and most important ceremonies were held at the Midwinter or New Year Festival. This was a time of cleansing and preparation for the new year that was about to begin.

False Face Society mask.

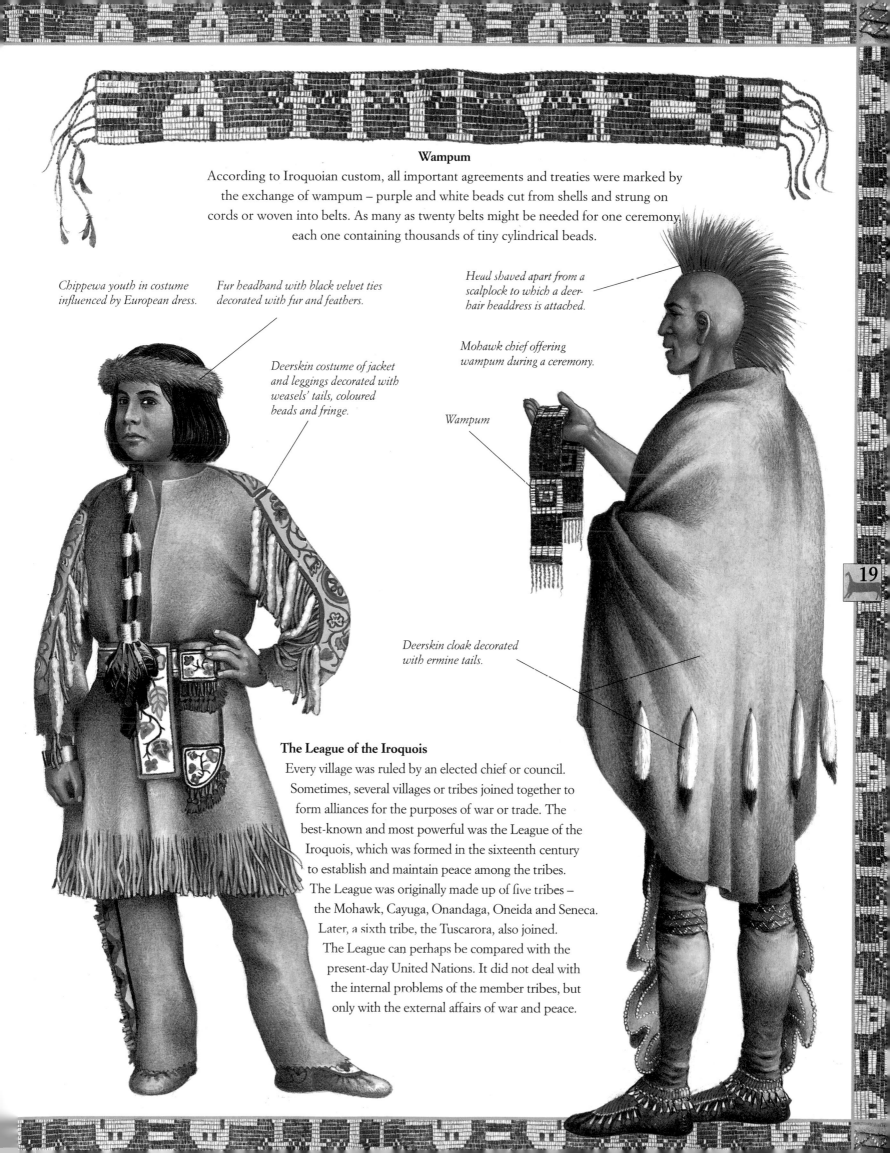

Wampum

According to Iroquoian custom, all important agreements and treaties were marked by the exchange of wampum – purple and white beads cut from shells and strung on cords or woven into belts. As many as twenty belts might be needed for one ceremony, each one containing thousands of tiny cylindrical beads.

Chippewa youth in costume influenced by European dress.

Fur headband with black velvet ties decorated with fur and feathers.

Head shaved apart from a scalplock to which a deer-hair headdress is attached.

Deerskin costume of jacket and leggings decorated with weasels' tails, coloured beads and fringe.

Mohawk chief offering wampum during a ceremony.

Wampum

Deerskin cloak decorated with ermine tails.

The League of the Iroquois

Every village was ruled by an elected chief or council. Sometimes, several villages or tribes joined together to form alliances for the purposes of war or trade. The best-known and most powerful was the League of the Iroquois, which was formed in the sixteenth century to establish and maintain peace among the tribes. The League was originally made up of five tribes – the Mohawk, Cayuga, Onandaga, Oneida and Seneca. Later, a sixth tribe, the Tuscarora, also joined. The League can perhaps be compared with the present-day United Nations. It did not deal with the internal problems of the member tribes, but only with the external affairs of war and peace.

Bordering Iroquoian territory and stretching southwards along the Atlantic coast were the villages of the Algonquian tribes, including the Shawnee, Ojibwa, Micmac, Delaware and Powhatan. They lived in wigwams – domed or conical frameworks of bent poles covered with sheets of bark or rush mats. Although most of the Algonquians did some farming, hunting and fishing were often more important. Some lived in villages only during the summer, abandoning them in the autumn to go in search of deer, elk, bear, beaver and muskrat. Some of the Algonquians who lived around the western Great Lakes moved out on to the prairies in the autumn to hunt buffalo.

The woods provided most of the raw materials that people needed to build and furnish their homes and to make tools and equipment. Whole trees were felled if large, thick sheets were wanted. Wigwams needed at least two such sheets in summer and a double thickness was needed in winter. Smaller pieces, used to make boxes and bowls, could be cut from a standing tree without damaging it.

Iroquois war club. The handle is carved in the shape of an animal head.

Building a Canoe
A canoe was made from sheets of birch bark, fitted over a cedarwood frame. The seams were stitched with spruce roots and painted with pine gum to make them watertight. As many as nine layers of bark could be peeled from a single birch tree.

The village was the centre of all activity, although in summer the men were often away on hunting, trading or war expeditions, while the women stayed to tend the crops. The fields around the village were worked until the soil was exhausted. The old village was then abandoned and a new one built several kilometres away. The woods around the new village were cleared by burning and new fields were prepared and planted. In about ten or twenty years time, when these fields in turn became exhausted, the cycle of moving and rebuilding began again.

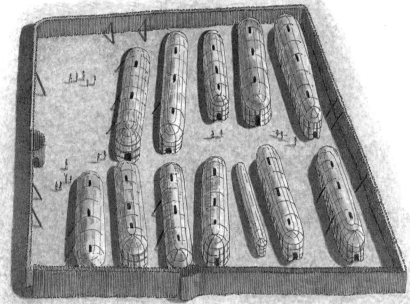

An Iroquois Village

A village consisted of rows of longhouses, constructed from stout wooden poles and roofed with sheets of bark. Each longhouse, on average around 25 metres in length and 6 to 7 metres wide, might be home to as many as twenty related families.

An Iroquois Longhouse

Within a communal longhouse, each family had its own private space partitioned off from the others. It contained a raised platform covered with reed mats or deerskins which was used as a seat or working area during the day and as a bed at night. Along the centre of the longhouse there was a series of fires for cooking, each one shared by the family on either side. Firewood, food and supplies were stored at the ends of the longhouse and corn cobs, dried meat and fish were hung from the roof.

Huron moccasins.

THE NORTHERN FORESTS

South of the Arctic and stretching across North America from the Labrador Coast almost as far as the Pacific is a vast area of dense forest and barren tundra. Here the summers, though warm, are very short, and the winters long and bitterly cold. For the Native Americans who lived in this subarctic region, life could be very hard, especially during the long winter months when food was scarce. Since it was too cold here for farming, people depended on what they caught by hunting, trapping or fishing. If hunters were unsuccessful, they and their families went hungry and could even starve to death.

Scoop used to remove ice from fishing holes.

Naskapi woman's ear ornaments.

Clothing

Shirts, parkas, trousers, leggings and moccasins were all made from caribou skin, with the fur left on if intended for winter wear. Eight or ten caribou skins might be needed to make a complete set of clothing for one person, and a pair of moccasins lasted only a few weeks. So not only were the hunters kept busy, their wives were too – cleaning and scraping the skins, smoking them to make them waterproof, then cutting and stitching them into garments for the whole family.

Hunting

Because animals were so important for survival, people developed strict rules for hunting them and for disposing of their remains. These rules were intended to show honour and respect to the animals so that they would allow themselves to be hunted. Moose and caribou antlers were decorated with ribbons and placed on specially-built racks. Bears' skulls were painted with special designs and tied to a tree overlooking water, since hunters believed that this would please the spirits of the dead bears. Rules also applied to the weapons and equipment used by hunters – even to the clothes they wore. Naskapi hunters wore special caribou-skin coats painted with intricate patterns, which were believed to have the power to attract the caribou herds.

Painted mask of the Ingalik people. Used during Mask Dance ceremonies.

Woman's costume with detachable cape and belt, in the style from around Great Slave Lake and along the Mackenzie River.

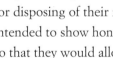

NORTHERN FORESTS

The northern conifer forests cover the subarctic zone from eastern Canada to Alaska in the west.

Travel and Transport

More skins, or sometimes sheets of bark, were needed as tent coverings. Because of the never-ending quest for food, people were always on the move, travelling in small family groups. They needed light, portable shelters that could be quickly and easily packed up. Many families travelled on foot, carrying their possessions on their backs. Some travelled by birch-bark canoe for as long as the waterways remained open and free from ice. Snowshoes were indispensable for winter hunting. Made of wooden frames bent into shape and laced with thin-cut strips of rawhide, they enabled the wearer to move over the deep, soft snow of the forests without sinking. Toboggans, drawn by hand or by teams of dogs, were used to carry heavier goods and supplies. Toboggans were made of pliable boards of birch or larch, turned up in front so that they could glide more easily over the snow. Dog teams were increasingly important as hunters became more involved in the fur trade and needed to transport their valuable furs to the trading posts. As well as their use in hunting, a team of six or eight dogs could haul a laden toboggan 30 or 40 kilometres a day.

Snowshoes.

Woman carrying a basket for collecting seeds. Her hat is also made of basketry.

THE PLATEAU AND BASIN

The people of the Plateau had much in common with their neighbours on the Plains, especially after they acquired horses in the early eighteenth century. Being able to travel further afield with horses, they came into contact with the Plains tribes and adopted many of their ways. Some of the Plateau tribes became skilful breeders and traders of horses, and took great pride in decking their mounts with colourful beaded trappings.

Food was relatively plentiful in this area. The rivers teemed with fish, especially salmon, which were speared, netted and trapped. Otters and beavers were trapped both for their meat and their fur, and hunters tracked herds of deer, antelope and mountain sheep. Basketfuls of edible plants, roots, fruit and nuts were collected. By contrast, the Great Basin to the south was an arid and desolate area which, even today, is thinly populated. With sparse vegetation and little animal life, it is small wonder that early explorers named it the 'Great American Desert'.

For those who lived here, starvation was a constant threat. Yet people did manage to survive by making the best possible use of the meagre resources available. Families joined forces to comb the territory – collecting grass seeds and nuts, digging for roots and bulbs, hunting antelope, rabbits, rats, lizards and insects. In spring they made bird-shaped decoys from reeds and feathers to lure migrating ducks to where hunters lay in wait.

Drum made of rawhide stretched over a wooden frame and painted with a design depicting a buffalo head and hooves. This drum was probably used in a dance or ceremony intended to bring good luck in hunting buffalo.

Decoy for hunting ducks. These were floated in marshes and lakes to lure migrating birds to where hunters lay in wait.

Surviving in the Great Basin

People living in the Great Basin used the vegetation available to build shelters and to make the equipment they needed to collect and process their food supply. The women of the Great Basin were expert basketmakers and produced a whole range of woven baskets designed for specialist tasks. There were fan-shaped beaters for dislodging seeds from grass-stems, trays for gathering, sorting, and winnowing seeds and nuts, larger baskets for storing them, and basketry bowls, waterproofed with pitch, for cooking and eating.

Although people were constantly moving in search of food, it was not an aimless search. They knew their own territory well and how to exploit it during the different seasons. They were prepared for hardship and at each camp-site they left hidden stores – supplies of flour, dried meat and berries – ready for their next visit.

The arrival of white settlers and the discovery of gold in the nineteenth century drastically affected the fragile way of life of these people and in the end destroyed it forever.

Elaborate masks were made for a favourite horse to wear on special occasions.

THE PLATEAU AND BASIN

The region known as the High Plateau is bounded by the Cascade Mountains on the west and by the Rockies to the east, and takes in parts of British Columbia, Washington, Oregon, Idaho and Montana. The Great Basin lies to the south and includes Nevada and Utah and parts of California, Oregon, Idaho, Wyoming and Colorado.

25

The Nez Perce were particularly noted for their breeding of the Appaloosa horse with its distinctive spotted coat.

CALIFORNIA

Before Europeans arrived in the late eighteenth century, California was one of the most densely populated areas of North America. Over sixty small, scattered tribes lived here in a land rich in natural resources.

Some of the northern Californian tribes, such as the Yurok, Karok and Hupa, had a way of life similar to their North-West Coast neighbours. Like them, they built large plank houses and went to sea in dug-out canoes. Here, as further north, wealth and status were important. Because food was plentiful, people had the leisure and means to hoard riches – prized furs and birdskins, knives finely flaked from obsidian and strings of the white dentalium or tooth shells, which were used as currency all along the coast.

Baskets intended as gifts or for use in ceremonies were richly decorated, covered entirely with bright iridescent feathers and hung with beads and shells. Such prized baskets were often buried in graves or burned at mourning ceremonies to honour the dead.

Strings of dentalium shell money were stored for safekeeping in purses carved from elk antler. The shells were graded according to length and appearance and the best were decorated with engraving and tufts of feathers to make them even more valuable. The value of most things was reckoned in dentalium shells. A house, for example, might be valued at three strings.

Basketry

Californian women made some of the finest baskets in the world. Baskets were made in many forms and used for a variety of purposes – for gathering, transporting and storing food and supplies, for wearing as hats and for cradling babies. Those made for cooking and serving food were so tightly woven that they could hold water without being waterproofed.

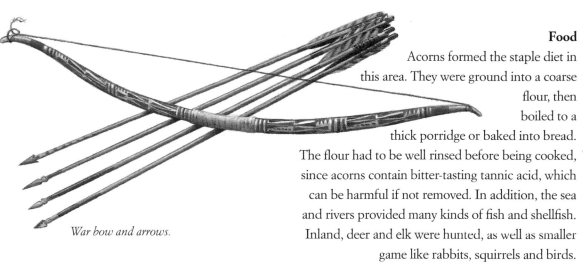
War bow and arrows.

Food

Acorns formed the staple diet in this area. They were ground into a coarse flour, then boiled to a thick porridge or baked into bread. The flour had to be well rinsed before being cooked, since acorns contain bitter-tasting tannic acid, which can be harmful if not removed. In addition, the sea and rivers provided many kinds of fish and shellfish. Inland, deer and elk were hunted, as well as smaller game like rabbits, squirrels and birds.

CALIFORNIA

To the west of the Great Basin, between the Sierra Nevada and the Pacific, lies California.

The End of a Way of Life

Towards the end of the eighteenth century, Spanish missionaries moved into central California and set up a chain of mission stations along the coast. As a result of the Indians' involvement with the missions, their traditional way of life began to come to an end. It was destroyed completely in the nineteenth century by the 1849 Californian gold rush, which led to brutal confrontations between the miners and the Indians who lived in the foothills of the Sierra Nevada and along the northern rivers. By 1870, more than 50,000 Indians had died from gunshot wounds, disease and starvation.

Dance headdress made of deerskin and decorated with feathers.

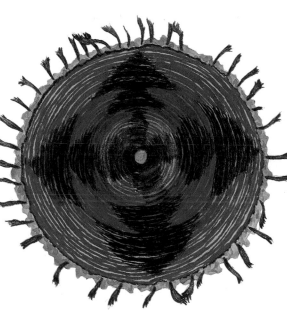

House built of bent poles and thatched with reeds.

The Simple Life

White settlers were often contemptuous of the native Californians, labelling them 'Diggers', because of their habit of digging for edible roots. It is true that the Californians' lifestyle was simple. They wore little clothing and their homes were roughly built brush shelters. But, when they held their elaborate ceremonies and dances, they wore costumes of softest deerskin decorated with brilliantly coloured feathers and shimmering abalone shell.

THE NORTH-WEST COAST

The people of the North-West Pacific Coast lived in small villages scattered along a steep and rugged coastline stretching nearly 1,800 kilometres from southern Alaska to northern California. The Tlingit, Tsimshian, Kwakiutl and Salish lived on the mainland. On the Queen Charlotte Islands were the Haida, and on Vancouver Island, the Nootka.

Food

Large sea creatures – seals, sea lions and porpoises – were hunted with harpoons. Special canoes were built for sea-hunting. These were smaller and narrower than those built for trade or war. Their hulls rubbed to a glassy smoothness, they slid though the water swiftly and silently, taking their prey by surprise. Perhaps the most spectacular sea-hunting exploits were those of the Nootka, who were intrepid master whalers. In their great dug-out canoes, the eight-man crews pursued and harpooned whales in the open seas.

Halibut hook.

THE NORTH-WEST COAST

Among the peoples of the North-West Coast, great importance was placed on social rank and status. Chiefs were at the top of the social system. Their houses were usually large enough to shelter four or five families, and those who lived with the chief made up the middle ranks of society. At the bottom of the system were the slaves – usually war captives or people traded from other tribes. They did the menial tasks of the household and were completely at the mercy of their owners.

Social status was largely based on wealth – counted in terms of canoes, carved boxes, fine clothing, slaves, even food. The natural resources of the area were such that many people were able to amass wealth of this sort. Although they hunted deer, goats and bears on the mountains and collected fruit and berries in the forest, the North-West Coast people were first and foremost fishermen.

Salmon

The sea and rivers provided the people of the North-West Coast with a huge variety of fish and shellfish. Salmon was the mainstay. Every year, vast numbers of migrating Pacific salmon returned from the sea to spawn in their native rivers. Traps, constructed like great baskets, were set up in the rivers and at points along the coast where the salmon gathered. A few weeks of feverish activity at these sites with nets and harpoons yielded enough salmon – filleted, smoked and stored – to keep entire villages fed throughout the stormy winter months. Special ceremonies were held to welcome the first salmon caught at each site. People believed that if the salmon were treated with honour and their bones returned reverently to the water, they would make the sacrificial run again the following year.

The towering forests of cedar and spruce provided the tribes with nearly all their raw materials. Standing up to 70 metres tall and often 2 metres or more in diameter, the cedar has a straight-grained wood, which can be split into long planks. It also has a soft, shaggy bark, which on the North-West Coast was used to make clothing, rope or mats. For some purposes the tree did not have to be chopped down. Planks could be split and bark stripped in long sheets from a standing tree. The coastal forests still contain living trees from which bark was stripped or planks split off over a century ago.

Mask representing Saiswei, a mythical being who lives in lakes.

Totems

Crest or 'totem' poles were carved and raised for many different purposes. The carvings, depicting supernatural animals and beings, represented legendary events in the history of the owner's family. Some were free-standing, while others were fixed on to the fronts of houses. Sometimes, the entrance to the house was carved at the base of the pole as a gaping mouth or beak. Some poles commemorated people or events, while others were mortuary poles, supporting the coffins of important people.

Ceremonies and Dances

Winter was the season for the most spectacular ceremonies and dances. To the rhythmic background of whistles and drums, costumed figures in fantastic masks crouched and whirled in the flickering firelight, imitating birds, animals and monsters. Speaking tubes hidden in the walls brought ghostly voices out of the darkness. The dancers swung through the air on ropes as if flying or suddenly vanished through concealed trapdoors.

Craft

Before they obtained metal tools from white traders, crafts people worked with adzes and chisels of polished stone, bone and shell, wedges of wood and antler, driven by heavy stone mauls, drills with bone or stone points and small carving tools made from the sharp incisor teeth of beavers or porcupines. With such tools, they built their great plank houses and hollowed out sea-going canoes 20 metres long, from a single log.

Mask representing a cannibal bird which, according to legend, preys on human beings, cracking open their skulls with its great beak. This mask was worn by a dancer at winter ceremonies.

Ceremonial hat worn by the host at potlatches. Each ring on the crown represents a potlatch given by the wearer.

Headdress consisting of a small wooden mask, carved and painted, and attached to a crown of sea lion whiskers, hung with ermine skins.

Dancing blanket made from cedar bark and mountain goat wool. The designs represent mythical beings associated with the owner's family.

Fringed skin apron.

Chief wearing ceremonial costume.

Potlatch

The North-West Coast people carved or painted crests on canoes and paddles, feast dishes, ceremonial clothing and a whole range of furnishings and utensils. All such items represented the wealth of their owner, and the most successful way for him to display his wealth was to hold a potlatch. This was an elaborate ceremonial feast, lasting several days, to which hundreds of guests might be invited. A potlatch was usually held to mark a family event, such as a marriage or death. But it was really a way for the host to demonstrate his wealth by distributing it among his guests or even destroying it. The more he gave away, and the longer the potlatch lasted, the more successful it was judged to be and the more the host's standing was enhanced.

Mask representing Tsonoqua, a mythical monster who lives in the forests and eats children.

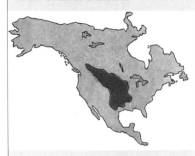

The Indians of the Great Plains occupied the area between the Mississippi River and the Rocky Mountains, including parts of the USA and Canada. The plains were huge grasslands stretching from northern Alberta and Saskatchewan in Canada to the Rio Grande border of Texas.

THE GREAT PLAINS

The Native Americans who lived on the Great Plains during the nineteenth century were of many tribes with different customs and different languages. The High Plains to the west was the territory of the nomadic tribes, such as the Blackfoot and Comanche, who lived almost entirely by hunting and who moved their camps with the movements of the game herds. On the eastern prairies were the settled village tribes, such as the Mandan and the Pawnee, who were farmers, but who rode out to the High Plains to hunt buffalo once or twice a year. What united them all was their dependence, to a greater or lesser degree, on the buffalo for food, clothing and shelter, and on the horse for travel and transport.

Sioux woman's dress made from two deerskins stitched together at the sides and shoulders. The cape-like sleeves are formed from the animals' hind legs. As glass trade beads became more readily available, dresses became more heavily decorated. By the 1870s, the entire bodice was often completely covered with beadwork. Sometimes, as here, the dress was worn with a leather belt decorated with metal discs. This style of costume is still worn today on special occasions.

Cradle in the form of a skin bag attached to a wooden frame so that it could be carried on the mother's back or saddle, or leaned against a tree or tipi.

Horses

Horses had become extinct in America at the end of the Ice Age, but they were reintroduced by Spanish explorers in the sixteenth century. By the beginning of the eighteenth century they had spread to the Plains. Horses were able to carry much heavier loads than the Indians' previous pack animal, the dog – perhaps around 135 kilograms compared with the 18 to 20 kilograms which a dog could manage. Dogs had been trained to drag a travois, a sort of V-shaped sledge, often made from two tipi poles lashed together. Now the travois was enlarged to suit the horse which meant that people could carry far greater quantities of food, clothing and equipment with them.

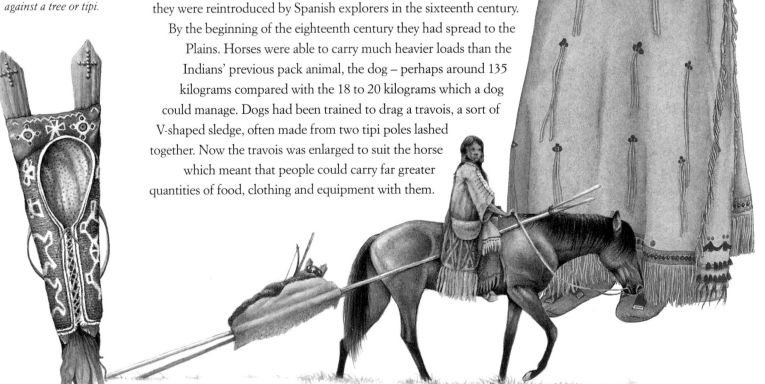

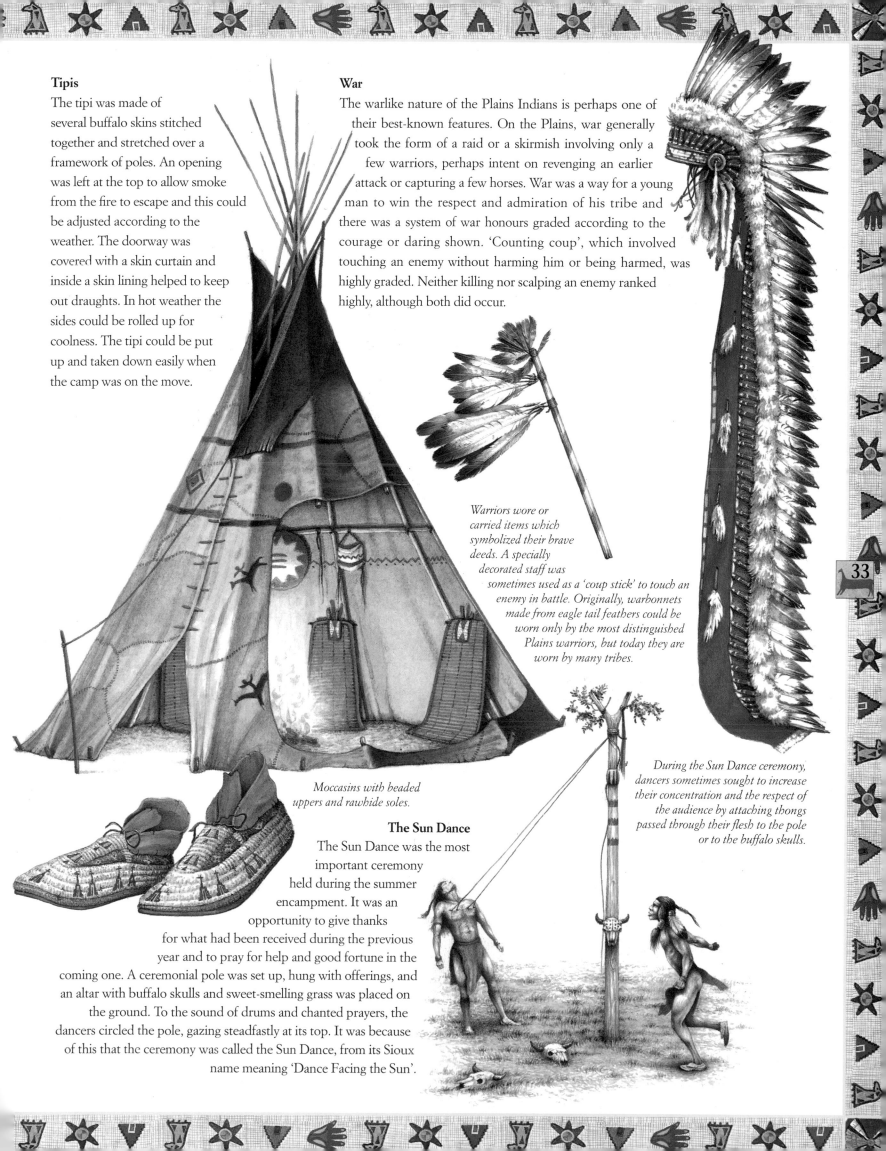

Tipis

The tipi was made of several buffalo skins stitched together and stretched over a framework of poles. An opening was left at the top to allow smoke from the fire to escape and this could be adjusted according to the weather. The doorway was covered with a skin curtain and inside a skin lining helped to keep out draughts. In hot weather the sides could be rolled up for coolness. The tipi could be put up and taken down easily when the camp was on the move.

War

The warlike nature of the Plains Indians is perhaps one of their best-known features. On the Plains, war generally took the form of a raid or a skirmish involving only a few warriors, perhaps intent on revenging an earlier attack or capturing a few horses. War was a way for a young man to win the respect and admiration of his tribe and there was a system of war honours graded according to the courage or daring shown. 'Counting coup', which involved touching an enemy without harming him or being harmed, was highly graded. Neither killing nor scalping an enemy ranked highly, although both did occur.

Warriors wore or carried items which symbolized their brave deeds. A specially decorated staff was sometimes used as a 'coup stick' to touch an enemy in battle. Originally, warbonnets made from eagle tail feathers could be worn only by the most distinguished Plains warriors, but today they are worn by many tribes.

33

Moccasins with beaded uppers and rawhide soles.

During the Sun Dance ceremony, dancers sometimes sought to increase their concentration and the respect of the audience by attaching thongs passed through their flesh to the pole or to the buffalo skulls.

The Sun Dance

The Sun Dance was the most important ceremony held during the summer encampment. It was an opportunity to give thanks for what had been received during the previous year and to pray for help and good fortune in the coming one. A ceremonial pole was set up, hung with offerings, and an altar with buffalo skulls and sweet-smelling grass was placed on the ground. To the sound of drums and chanted prayers, the dancers circled the pole, gazing steadfastly at its top. It was because of this that the ceremony was called the Sun Dance, from its Sioux name meaning 'Dance Facing the Sun'.

Paintings were made on skin to record important events and ceremonies.

Storage box made of painted rawhide.

Bone tool with a metal blade used for cleaning skins.

Summer Meetings

The summer encampment was the only time in the year when an entire tribe gathered together in the form of a camp circle. This was the time for tribal business, council meetings and important ceremonies. It was also an exciting social occasion, an opportunity to meet friends, arrange marriages and join in sports and games. Everyone wore their best finery. Horses were decked out in elaborate trappings and the warriors rode in proud procession through the camp displaying their weapons and shields.

Dance rattle made from wood and rawhide.

Hunting Buffalo

Buffalo were hunted throughout the year, but ways of hunting varied with the season. While hunters did sometimes stalk buffalo on their own or in small groups, it was more common for a large number of hunters to join together to attack a whole herd. In autumn and winter, the hunters continued to use the prehistoric method of driving the herd over a cliff or into a specially constructed enclosure to be slaughtered, although now it was done on horseback rather than on foot as before.

During the summer, when the buffalo spread out over the Plains, two methods were used. In the first, a group of hunters on horseback surrounded a buffalo herd and shot the animals down as they milled in confusion. The second involved a headlong charge by mounted hunters running alongside the buffalo and picking off selected animals at close quarters. Bows and arrows were generally preferred to guns for hunting, since early guns were difficult to reload on a fast-moving horse, and were often inaccurate and expensive.

Hoe with a wooden handle and blade made from the shoulder bone of an elk or buffalo.

The design painted on a shield was believed to give protection to its owner, who usually received inspiration for the design in a dream.

Farmers

The farming tribes lived in tipis when they went to hunt buffalo on the Plains in summer, but the rest of the year they spent in their villages of earth-lodges, which were large dome-shaped structures of wood covered with turf. In their nearby fields, they grew corn, beans, squash and melons, some of which they traded with the nomadic tribes in exchange for meat and skins.

Buffalo

Almost every part of the buffalo was used in some way. The meat was eaten fresh or else dried and stored for winter. The skins were cleaned and dried to make tough rawhide for storage boxes, saddle-bags, riding tackle and ropes. Dressed and softened, the skins were made into clothing and bedding, covers for tipis and saddle-blankets. The bones of the buffalo were turned into tools, its horns into cups and ladles, its sinews into sewing thread and bow-strings. Buffalo fat was used as a polish or, mixed with coloured earth, as paint. Its hooves were boiled to make glue and its dung collected for fuel.

THE SOUTH-WEST

The landscape of the South-West is one of the most dramatic in North America. The northern part is a high plateau of red sandstone worn by wind and water into fantastic pinnacles of rock, steep-sided mesas and deep canyons, while to the south lies a semi-desert, cut by mountains and slow-moving rivers. Because much of this desert and mountain land did not appeal to nineteenth-century white settlers, there was no removal of native people to reservations. Many of the Native Americans here continue to occupy the same lands as they did when Spanish explorers first arrived nearly 500 years ago. Some of their settlements (which the explorers called 'pueblos' – meaning villages) are in fact much older. The pueblo of Acoma, perched high on a mesa in New Mexico for over a thousand years, claims to be the oldest continuously inhabited town in the USA.

Pueblo Houses

Many Pueblo are descendants of the prehistoric Anasazi people and, like them, they live in homes of stone and adobe, built in terraced clusters around a central square. Like the Anasazi, they are farmers, growing fields of corn, beans, squash, melons, peaches and cotton, which they still spin and weave to make ceremonial clothing.

Like their Anasazi ancestors, the present-day Pueblo people are skilful potters. Most still work in the traditional way, building their pots by coiling and decorating them with natural colours once they have dried. Each Pueblo village has developed its own distinctive shapes and designs.

Pueblo Ceremonies

Because farming is often difficult in this arid land, the Pueblos have developed an annual round of ceremonies designed to bring rain and ensure good harvests. Kachinas play a major role. These are supernatural beings, impersonated in ceremonies by masked and costumed dancers. Some are the spirits of ancestors. Others are animal spirits or represent natural forces, such as wind and rain. Children are given wooden dolls, that are carved and painted in the form of kachinas, so that they can learn about the ceremonies.

Pottery

Many Pueblo potters are highly regarded as artists and their work is eagerly sought after.

The Pueblo people include the Hopi and Zuni in North-Eastern Arizona and western New Mexico with the Eastern Pueblos, such as Taos, San Ildefonso, Santo Domingo and Isleta, spread along the Rio Grande River in central New Mexico. While other Native American cultures have changed or disappeared, that of the Pueblos has proved very strong and resilient and in many ways their way of life seems to have changed little over the centuries.

THE SOUTH-WEST

South-West Indians of the Great Plains occupied the area between the Mississippi River and the Rocky Mountains, including parts of both the USA and Canada. The plains were grasslands stretching from northern Alberta and Saskatchewan in Canada to the Rio Grande border of Texas.

Food

Traditionally Pueblo farmers grew corn, beans and squash. Later they learned from the Spanish to plant wheat, melons, chilli peppers and fruit trees. Groups of hunters stalked deer and antelope and communal rabbit hunts were organized in most villages. The annual round of ceremonies still held today seeks to ensure plentiful rain for the crops and a continuing supply of game.

Hopi girl grinding corn meal using a stone roller on a stone slab. Her elaborate 'squash blossom' hairstyle showed that she was unmarried. Married women wore their hair in simple braids

Apache dancer impersonating one of the Gahan or Mountain Spirits who have the power to help or harm human beings. They wear towering wooden headdresses and carry wooden swords.

Apache

Compared with the Pueblos, the Apache are relative newcomers to the South-West. Small bands began to move into the area from the north during the fifteenth century. They were fierce raiders, attacking the peaceful Pueblos, stealing their produce, kidnapping women and children and disappearing into their hide-outs deep in remote canyons. Their name 'Apache' comes from a Pueblo word meaning 'enemy'. During the seventeenth century, while some of the Apache continued to roam the mountains and plains to the north, others began to settle down, for part of the year at least. They raised herds of sheep and goats and farmed the land like the Pueblos. They became known as the Apaches of the fields – 'Apaches del Nabahu' – the Navajo.

By the beginning of the nineteenth century, the Navajo people had moved into the area in Arizona which they regard as their traditional homeland and which is now part of the Navajo reservation. They did not live in towns like the Pueblos, but in groups of hogans – circular timber structures, pointed or domed, covered over with hard-packed earth. Usually several related families lived together and, as well as the hogans, the settlement also included outhouses, stores and pens for livestock. The Navajo remained semi-nomadic and spent the summer moving with their herds, returning to their hogans in winter.

Sandpainting

The Navajo have adopted Pueblo ceremonies, but developed them in their own way. Some of their most important ceremonies are concerned with curing sickness and disease. Such ceremonies often require the making of a sandpainting on the floor of the hogan. It is made by a shaman who depicts episodes from Navajo mythology in colours made from finely powdered sand, charcoal, cornmeal and pollen. The power of the sandpainting is used, together with other ceremonies, to restore the patient to health.

Crafts

Silverwork, set with turquoise and other semi-precious stones, began to be made by Navajo men in the late nineteenth century. Materials and designs were borrowed from their Mexican neighbours, but Navajo silversmiths adapted these designs in their own way. Their output included bridle ornaments, water bottles and tobacco boxes, as well as belts, necklaces, bracelets and rings which are still popular today.

Navajo bracelets made in silver and turquoise.

There are a great many curing ceremonies, each with its own songs and sandpaintings. Traditionally, a sandpainting is made on the floor of the hogan and can take several hours to complete. At the end of the ceremony, the sandpainting is destroyed.

There are several types of hogan. The oldest is the forked-stick hogan, built from a framework of poles covered with branches and plastered with mud. Nowadays, the six-sided hogan with log walls is most widely used. Whatever the form, however, Navajo mythology decrees that the doorway should always face towards the rising sun.

Traditional Navajo hair comb.

Spinning and Weaving

It was from the Pueblos that Navajo women learned to spin, dye and weave the wool from their sheep, producing hard-wearing patterned blankets which they used for clothing and bedding and to trade with other tribes for corn, meat and skins. Some of their fabrics were so finely woven that it was claimed they could be used to carry water. When trading posts were set up on the reservation during the second half of the nineteenth century, the white traders saw Navajo weaving as a valuable commodity. They supplied the weavers with coloured wool and yarn and packets of the new chemical dyes, which gave shades much brighter than those that could be obtained with the old natural dyes. They encouraged them to weave patterns more appealing to white customers and to change from their traditional light blankets to heavier rugs more suitable for floor coverings. Navajo rugs of this type are still woven in the traditional way and are highly prized by collectors.

NATIVE AMERICANS IN HISTORY

Hiawatha's diplomatic efforts brought peace to the warring Iroqois, at least for a time.

Hiawatha

Hiawatha was a sixteenth-century Mohawk chief who helped to set up the League of the Iroquois. To try to end the many years of intertribal fighting, Hiawatha visited each one of the tribes in turn, urging peace and unity. At a meeting attended by all the chiefs, the laws and customs of the League were laid down and agreed. Hiawatha was given an honoured place in the Great Council of the League. Colonists were much impressed by the workings of the League and many historians believe that the constitution of the USA may have been partly based on it. Longfellow's well-known poem, *The Song of Hiawatha*, is based on Algonquian legends and has nothing to do with the historical Hiawatha.

Wampum

Wampum belts, made of purple and white shell beads, were used to convey messages between tribes. White beads symbolized peace and friendship, while the purple variety indicated sorrow and death.

Powhatan

Powhatan's real name was Wahunsonacock, but the English colonists who settled in his territory in 1607 called him by the name of the tribes over whom he ruled in what is now Virginia. Although he viewed the colonists as threatening invaders, he helped them when they were in danger of starvation and for a year or so, relations between the Indians and the colonists ran smoothly. The colonists gave Powhatan the title of king and presented him with a crown sent from England.

In 1609, however, the colonists' aggressive demands led to the outbreak of war. The treacherous kidnapping of his daughter, Pocahontas, forced Powhatan to agree to peace in 1614. Weary and embittered, he gave up his leadership and died four years later.

Pocahontas

The daughter of Wahunsonacock, the powerful chief of the Powhatan people, Pocahontas was born about 1595. In 1607, Captain John Smith, the leader of the English colonists, was captured by the Powhatans, but later released. No one really knows the truth behind the well-known story of Captain Smith's life being saved by Pocahontas. The incident may have been made up by Captain Smith much later on.

In 1613, the colonists captured Pocahontas, offering to ransom her in exchange for English prisoners held by the Powhatans. Although the Indians released their prisoners, the colonists continued to hold Pocahontas. While still in captivity, she was converted to Christianity and renamed Rebecca. She fell in love with one of her captors, John Rolfe, and married him in 1614, their marriage sealing the peace between the colonists and the Powhatans.

Two years later, with her husband and baby son, she sailed to England, where she was received at court by King James I. Sadly, she was never to see her native land again. In 1617, while about to set out on the homeward journey, she became ill, probably with smallpox, and died at Gravesend, near London, aged only twenty-two.

After Powhatan's death war again broke out and the Indians were heavily defeated. By the mid-18th century, the Powhatan people had been almost completely destroyed by warfare and disease.

Fan

The most famous portrait painted of Pocahontas depicts her as an English noblewoman. The clothes she wears and the fan she carries are all of European manufacture and there is little to show that this is the daughter of a Native American chief.

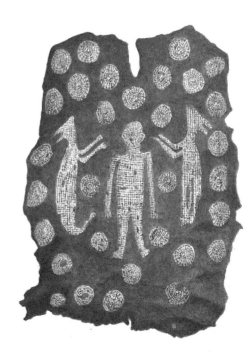

Mantle

Although traditionally known as Powhatan's mantle, this bead-decorated deerskin, brought to London in the early 17th century, may in fact have been a temple hanging.

Sequoyah

Sequoyah, who invented the Cherokee writing system, was born about 1760. Although he himself was poorly educated, he saw the usefulness of being able to express thoughts and ideas on paper and set about trying to put the Cherokee language into written form. In 1828, the tribe began to publish their own newspaper, the *Cherokee Phoenix*, printed both in Cherokee and English. Sequoyah died in 1843. The giant redwood tree found in California was named in his honour after his death.

Portrait of Sequoyah with his writing system.

Writing System

In spite of much discouragement and ridicule, Sequoyah persevered developing a writing system for twelve years. Finally, in 1821, he produced a set of eighty-six symbols, each one representing a different syllable in the Cherokee language. Within a few months, thousands of Cherokee men, women and children had learned to read and write using Sequoyah's system.

Nekt

According to Tsimshian tradition, Nekt was a powerful warrior chief who raided the villages of the North-West Coast from his hill-fort overlooking the Kitwanga River. He is said to have built the fort according to instructions received in a dream. The palisade was equipped with a system of large spiked logs which could be rolled down on attackers. If the fort was captured, underground hiding places linked to trapdoors enabled the occupants to escape through tunnels underneath the palisade. Local legend claims that, during an attack on the fort, Nekt was killed by a bullet fired from the first gun ever seen in the area.

Portrait of Nekt.
The archaeological evidence does suggest that the stories about Nekt are based on historical fact and that he himself was a real-life character.

The Hill-Fort on the Kitwanga River

In 1979, archaeologists excavating the site of the Kitwanga hill-fort found the remains of several large buildings surrounded by a palisade. Inside the palisade they found over a thousand large pits, where dried fish, meat and berries had been stored, presumably in case of siege. They also discovered a number of smaller pits, apparently designed as hiding places and equipped with trapdoors. Further evidence showed that the site had been burned and abandoned about 1830, just around the time when the first trading posts in the area were being set up, making guns readily available. This is also the time when tradition claims that Nekt was killed and his fort burned by his enemies.

Sacagewa

Sacagewa (meaning Bird Woman) was a Shoshone woman who accompanied the explorers Lewis and Clark on their epic journey from the Mississippi River to the Pacific Coast at the beginning of the nineteenth century. Born about 1785, Sacagewa was captured at the age of twelve by a Crow raiding party and sold as a slave to the Mandan, who lived on the Upper Missouri River on the other side of the Rocky Mountains. In November 1804, the Lewis and Clark expedition stopped to winter among the Mandan and recruited Sacagewa and her husband, a French trapper, to join them on the next leg of their journey. When they at last set out in April 1805, Sacagewa was carrying her two-month-old baby son. With her local knowledge of the area, she proved extremely useful as a guide and interpreter, and was particularly successful in obtaining supplies from the tribes encountered on the way. One Nez Perce chief told Lewis and Clark that it was only the sight of Sacagewa in their canoe that guaranteed them a friendly welcome. On the return journey the following year, the expedition passed through Shoshone territory and Sacagewa was reunited with her family, who had long ago believed her dead. She is said to have returned to the Mandan village at the end of the expedition and died in 1884, at the age of ninety-eight.

Little is known of Sacagewa's life or that of her son after the end of the expedition.

43

Cradle

Sacagewa may have carried her baby in a cradle similar to this one, which is made of wood covered with buckskin. During the journey, the baby would have been laced into the cradle and carried on his mother's back.

Wrist Guard

Navajo archers wore a leather band called a ketoh to protect their wrists from the bowstring. During the 19th century, they began to attach silver plates to the leather. Although ketohs are no longer used as wrist guards, they are still made and worn as items of jewellery.

Manuelito

In 1851, the United States army built and occupied Fort Defiance in New Mexico Territory in the heart of Navajo country. As a result, the Navajo found their herds of sheep and goats competing for precious pasture with the horses, mules and cattle brought in by the army. Tension grew between the two sides and came to a head when some of the soldiers shot Manuelito's livestock and burned his village. The following year, a band of Navajo, led by Manuelito, attacked Fort Defiance and almost overran it, before being driven off.

Dahaana Baadaani, known as Manuelito, was the Navajo war chief who, for twenty-five years, led resistance to white encroachment on his lands.

The outbreak of the American Civil War in 1861 led to the troops being withdrawn to the battlefront and the Navajo took advantage of their absence to step up their raids on the white settlements in the area. In retaliation, the government ordered a 'scorched earth' campaign against the Navajo, destroying their homes, fields and herds, and killing those who resisted. Many Navajo surrendered and were taken to a distant reservation. Manuelito and his followers continued to hold out in the mountains until 1866 when, exhausted and starving, they too were forced to surrender.

Conditions on the reservation were very poor and many people died from hunger and disease. Finally, in 1868, a peace treaty was drawn up and the Navajo were allowed to return to their homeland, now designated a reservation. Manuelito, who continued to play an important part in helping his people to rebuild their lives, died in 1893.

Sitting Bull

Sitting Bull took an active part in the wars against the white settlers on the Plains throughout most of the 1860s and 1870s. In 1876, his refusal to go with his followers to a reservation led the army to mount a campaign against the Sioux which resulted in the defeat of Colonel Custer's troops at the Battle of the Little Bighorn. This defeat, coming just as the USA were celebrating the centenary of the Declaration of American Independence, was seen by the government as a humiliation and one which they were determined to avenge. The Indians were relentlessly hunted down and, by 1881, all the warring Plains tribes had been forced into reservations. Sitting Bull had fled to Canada after the Battle of the Little Bighorn. When he returned, he was arrested and jailed for two years. On his release, he too was sent to the reservation.

In 1890, a movement known as the Ghost Dance spread across the Plains, promising the Indians that the old ways would return. Although its message was essentially peaceful, the government feared that it would provoke an uprising and that Sitting Bull might become involved. They ordered him to be imprisoned, but, in the course of his arrest, Sitting Bull was shot dead. Two weeks after his death, the army, still nervous about the possible effects of the Ghost Dance, opened fire on a group of Sioux, killing two hundred men, women and children. This massacre, at a place called Wounded Knee, has become a powerful image for all Native Americans, as has Sitting Bull himself.

Bag

Beaded buckskin bags were used by tribal leaders to store their formal smoking equipment. The pipe bowl was removed from the stem and placed in the bag along with the tobacco and the tamper used to pack the tobacco into the pipe bowl.

Tatanka Yotanka, whose name is usually translated as Sitting Bull, was a Sioux shaman and war chief.

Calumet

Plains tribes regarded calumets (ceremonial pipes) as highly sacred. Such pipes were smoked during ceremonies to solemnise important decisions or to seal treaties. Most pipe bowls were carved from catlinite, a distinctive red stone obtained from a quarry in Minnesota.

GLOSSARY

Adobe
A Spanish word for sun-dried clay bricks.

Conquistadors
A Spanish word meaning 'conquerors'. It usually refers to the Spanish conquerors of America in the 16th century.

Hogan
A Navajo house built of wood covered with earth.

Ice Age
A time when large areas of the earth were covered with ice.

Kachina
A supernatural being in Pueblo mythology.

Kiva
An underground room in Pueblo villages used for ceremonies and meetings.

Lacrosse
A game in which players use long-handled rackets to catch and throw the ball.

Litter
A bed or couch mounted on two poles and carried at each end on men's shoulders.

Mastodon
A large elephant-like animal now extinct.

Mesa
A steep-sided flat-topped mountain.

Mica
A type of rock which can be split into thin, transparent sheets.

Nomadic
A term used to describe people who move from place to place, usually in search of food.

Palisade
A fence of wooden stakes.

Pemmican
Dried meat pounded into powder and mixed with fat and berries. It could be stored away until needed.

Potlatch
A special feast held to celebrate an important event and to exchange gifts.

Rawhide
Hide which has been cleaned but not softened. Unlike buckskin, which has been softened by tanning, rawhide is hard and stiff.

Sandpainting
A design made by sprinkling powdered colours onto a bed of sand and used in special ceremonies.

Shaman
Someone with special powers to communicate with the spirits and cure sickness.

Snowshoe
A round or oval wooden frame laced with hide strips. People wear these strapped to their feet to help them walk over the surface of snow.

Tipi
A conical tent made of wooden poles covered with buffalo skins or (by the end of the 19th century) canvas.

Toboggan
A type of sledge.

Travois
A framework made of two long poles (often tipi poles) tied together at one end. Pulled by dogs or horses, it was used to transport goods. It had no wheels and the ends of the poles dragged along the ground.

Tundra
A cold treeless area.

Wampum
Shell beads strung together and used as gifts or money.

Wigwam
A dome-shaped shelter made of bent poles covered with skins or bark.

PLACES TO VISIT

The following museums all have collections of Native American objects. They may not always have them on display, however, and you should check with each museum before you visit to find out what you will be able to see.

Aberdeen
Marischal Museum
Marischal College
Aberdeen AB9 1AS
Tel: 01224 273131

Belfast
Ulster Museum
Botanic Gardens
Belfast BT9 5AB
Tel: 01232 381251/8

Birmingham
Birmingham Museum and
Art Gallery
Chamberlain Square
Birmingham B3 3DH
Tel: 0121 2352834

Brighton
Brighton Museum and Art Gallery
4/5 Pavilion Buildings
Brighton BN1 1EE
Tel: 01273 603005

Bristol
Bristol Museum and Art Gallery
Queen's Road
Bristol BS8 1RL
Tel: 01179 223571

Cambridge
University Museum of Archaeology
and Anthropology
Downing Street
Cambridge CNB2 3DZ
Tel: 01223 337733/333516

Dundee
Dundee Art Galleries and Museum
Albert Square
Dundee DD1 1DA
Tel: 01382 432020

Edinburgh
National Museums of Scotland
Chambers Street
Edinburgh EH1 1JF
Tel: 01312 257534

Exeter
Royal Albert Memorial Museum
Queen Street
Exeter EX4 3RX
Tel: 01392 265858

Glasgow
Hunterian Museum
University of Glasgow
Glasgow G12 8QQ
Tel: 01413 304221

Glasgow
Glasgow Art Gallery
and Museum
Kelvingrove
Glasgow G3 8AG
Tel: 01412 872000

Hastings
Hastings Museum
and Art Gallery
Cambridge Road
Hastings TN34 1ET
Tel: 01424 781155

Ipswich
Ipswich Museum
High Street
Ipswich IP1 3QH
Tel: 01473 254246

Leeds
Leeds City Museum
Calverley Street
Leeds LS1 3AA
Tel: 01532 478279

Liverpool
Liverpool Museum
William Brown Street
Liverpool L3 8EN
Tel: 0151 2070001

London
Horniman Museum
London Road
London SE22 3PQ
Tel: 0181 6991872

London
The Museum of Mankind
Burlington Gardens
London W1X 2EX
Tel: 0171 3238043

Manchester
The Manchester Museum
University of Manchester
Oxford Road
Manchester M13 9PL
Tel: 0161 2752634

Oxford
Ashmolean Museum of Art
and Archaeology
Beaumont Street
Oxford OX1 2PH
Tel: 01865 278000

Oxford
Pitt Rivers Museum
South Parks Road
Oxford OX1 2PH
Tel: 01865 278000

Perth
Perth Museum and Art Gallery
George Street
Perth PH1 5LB
Tel: 01738 632488

Saffron Walden
Saffron Walden Museum
Museum Street
Saffron Walden CB10 1JL
Tel: 01799 510333

Sheffield
Sheffield City Museum
Weston Park
Sheffield S10 2TP
Tel: 01742 768588

INDEX